If I Onl

The Story

Sister Claudia

If I Only Love Jesus

The Story of Sister Claudia

Basilea Schlink

MARSHALL, MORGAN AND SCOTT
London

Marshall, Morgan & Scott
a member of the Pentos group
1 Bath Street, London EC1V 9LB

Copyright © Basilea Schlink 1973
First Published in Great Britain 1973
Fifth impression 1978

ISBN 0 551 05288 0

Printed in Great Britain by
Bowen & Court Ltd, Beckenham, Kent
8710L50

The Secret of a Transformation

Ward 6 in a modern multi-storied hospital—our Sister Claudia lay fatally ill. Though she was only 35,* she remained filled with lively cheerfulness even in this situation. She was the centre of the ward, everybody's favourite. The young nurses would cluster round her bed. They had probably very little contact with "religious" life. They came and admired the lovely, light-coloured Sister's dress, which Sister Claudia took from the wardrobe to show them.

But in fact it was something else which fascinated the nurses. Sister Claudia told them why this dress was so precious to her. She had worn it ever since she had consecrated herself to the One who had become her great love—Jesus. It was as though Jesus Christ Himself shone forth from her, attracting everyone. Her room seemed to have a magnetic power. Time and again the ward nurse would find an excuse to look in on her. And every day one of the doctors would sit by her bedside for half an hour to hear her speak of Jesus.

Sister Claudia—plagued by dreadful pain? Sister Claudia —a candidate for death? It did not seem so. Whenever she went for her check-ups—even though she was so weak —she would put on her Sisters' dress so that people would come up to her, and she would have the chance of giving a word of testimony.

She would take advantage of every opportunity to tell

*She was born on May 31st, 1935, in Württemberg, Germany, and entered the Sisterhood of Mary in 1958.

people about Jesus. At the beginning, when she was not yet so confined to bed, she would suddenly appear at the side of the very busy ward nurse and say with a friendly smile, "Is there anything I can do to help?" She asked us to send our sound slide series about the Sisterhood of Mary so that she could show it to the nurses in their off-duty period.

Sister Claudia was so weak and ill, suffering indescribable pains. She knew that she had only a few weeks more to live. Where did she find her strength? How was it that she was filled with such contagious joy? It would have greatly surprised anyone who had known her ten years before and not seen her since. For by nature Sister Claudia was not a strong personality, as we had discovered after she had come to live with us in the Mother House.

It was autumn, 1961. I was lying in bed, still recovering from a serious illness. I was not to be excited. No Sisters were allowed to come and see me. And yet I heard of someone pleading to come all the same. "Couldn't Sister Claudia come to you? She's crying so bitterly and she so much wants to speak to you."

Sister Claudia had recently made a seriously wrong decision, causing us much grief. She had no longer wanted to follow her calling. In a rash moment she left the Sisterhood. She did not want to accompany the Lord Jesus on His way of the cross. But after a very short while she had returned, weeping bitterly and desperately unhappy about herself.

As she sat beside me then, I asked her, "How could you have done this? Don't you love Jesus at all?"

She later confessed that that question had pierced her heart. Filled with pain, she realised that it was lack of love for Jesus that had driven her away. Sobbing, she told me,

"I want to love Him, no matter what it costs. May I begin again as a Sister of Mary?"

Should we take another chance? It was a serious decision to make.

We had often said, half jokingly, that Sister Claudia had "a restless nature"; she could never stay in any place for long without wanting to have a change. Wouldn't life in our Sisterhood, where we live only to love and glorify Jesus, and where every Sister is prepared to make sacrifices, be too hard for her? Would it not be too much to expect from her? When we commit ourselves completely to Jesus, we give up our own freedom and independence for His sake and for the sake of His commission, so that we are completely bound to Him and always available for Him. Would Sister Claudia be able to do this?

After the last experience, it didn't seem so. But here she was, full of penitence and begging for permission to come back to us. So I took her into my arms, prayed with her and blessed her and accepted her once more into our midst, trusting God and knowing that for Him nothing is impossible. I sensed at that moment that the Lord was at work in Sister Claudia, and that her repentance came from Him.

Mother Martyria and I trusted that He would continue to lead our Sister. Hadn't we already seen how the victorious power of the blood of Jesus can work in people to free them from their old self? Hadn't we seen such transformations in other Sisters who had come to us with a melancholy disposition and were now joyfully and steadfastly following Jesus? Couldn't the Lord work a miracle here also? That would bring glory to His name.

So we took the risk with Sister Claudia and let her work as a Garden Sister on our little Land of Canaan where we live. She was a nature lover, and we thought she would benefit from the fresh air and the sun, the flowers and meadows in the beautiful land of Canaan. We welcomed her back into the family of our Sisterhood, though not without some trepidation. When we met her we felt that there was so little of the radiance and the peace of Jesus in her face. Her countenance mirrored only earthly things. It was expressionless, the way it had struck us when she had first arrived three years before.

But shortly after her return to the Mother House something decisive happened. After a few weeks, when she came to talk to me, I could scarcely recognise her. Hadn't God promised to take away the stony heart and give in return a soft, tender heart, sensitive to sin? I was deeply moved as she once again wept so heart-rendingly over what she had done to Jesus. Was it merely the after-effect of the tears she had shed when she returned to us? No. During the course of the next few years, she came to me again and again—just as all my spiritual daughters do at certain intervals. But each time I was astonished. Each time a real "Claudia" came to me, for "Claudia" means "weeping". Each time she would weep for what she had done to Jesus and to us.

A miracle had occurred. Through the wrong decision she had made at the beginning of her life in our Sisterhood she had become a poor sinner. Now her face began to take on a new expression. If we imagine that people who are constantly sorrowing over their sin and living in repentance are tormenting themselves and must be depressed and unhappy, Sister Claudia's life teaches us differently. I grew more and more astonished as I saw how her tears brought forth joy and thanksgiving over the forgiveness of Jesus. Repentance was like a stream. New life was continually flowing forth—most of all, an intimate, fervent love for Jesus. It was the

8

"first love", which had now been given to her.

In the years which followed it became evident what a great change had taken place in our Sister. "When Sister Claudia is with us, she is radiant like the sun," the other Garden Sisters used to say. One day, in one of the farm buildings, they found a picture of the scourging of our Saviour. Written beneath it were the words, "Jesus is calling, 'Stay with Me in prayer!'" Sister Claudia had secretly put the picture there as a reminder to remain in fellowship with Jesus all day long. She could not bear to do her work separated from Jesus, and she realised that she and the other Garden Sisters were always open to this danger. It was her love for Jesus, born out of repentance, that made her so determined that He should become the centre of their lives.

One day she said to one of the other Garden Sisters: "Will you make a pact with me? We must pray every day that Jesus will receive more love, real praise and honour in our morning Bible studies and in the 'three o'clock prayer in remembrance of His suffering'!"

A fire burned in her heart: God must be loved. He must not be grieved by lukewarmness. So it is not surprising that one of the Sisters commented: "The prayer times with Sister Claudia were unforgettable. They were always something extraordinary. She was never spiritually tired. There was always repentance, dedication, fire and praise in her heart." More and more we could see the love of Jesus in her face. A spiritual radiance shone out from her.

There Is Power in the Blood of the Lamb

What lay behind such a transformation? What was the secret of her victory? One day when she was with me—I can still see her before my eyes—she made a request in such a heart-moving way: "I would love to have a prayer which praises the blood of Jesus, which I could always pray, because there is power in the blood of the Lamb. I have such a weak personality and I need the blood of the Lamb so much to overcome the attacks of the enemy and my sin!"

I gladly fulfilled Sister Claudia's request. When I gave her the piece of paper with this prayer in praise of the blood of Jesus, her face became radiant, and she hurried away as though she had received a precious treasure.

I praise the wounds and the blood of the Lamb*
   that heals the weakness of my body,
   that heals the weakness of my soul,
   that heals the weakness of my spirit!
Praise be to the blood of the Lamb*
   in His forgiving power,
   in His releasing power,
   in His victorious power,
   in His renewing power,
   in His protecting power.
For him who believes in the power of the blood of Jesus, nothing is impossible!

*to be repeated before every new declaration

I praise the blood of the Lamb*
    that covers all my sins so that they can no longer be seen,
    that cleanses me from all my sins and makes me white as
       snow,
    that has power to free me from all my bondages and
       chains of sin,
    that is stronger than my own sin-infested blood and
       remoulds me into the image of God,
    that is victorious over all powers that seek to oppress me,
       over every power of the enemy,
    and that prepares for me the bridal garment.
I praise the blood of the Lamb that makes all things new.
Hallelujah! Amen.

This prayer now came alive in the life of Sister Claudia.
She put it to good use, praying it daily with great fervour,
and when the other Sisters asked her how she was able to
overcome in the battle against sin, and why the enemy had
to yield, she showed them the prayer and passed it on to
them. Later, when she served in Italy and visited many of
the convents there and people asked her how she dealt with
her sins, she would tell them of the transforming power of
the blood of Jesus, and shared with them the prayer prais-
ing the blood of Jesus. So through her the prayer found its
way into the convents.

She took one sentence from the prayer and wrote it in
her diary, making it her own confession of faith: "For him
who believes in the power of the blood of Jesus, nothing is
impossible." This became more and more evident in her
life, especially after her bridal consecration on October
30th, 1966. The Sisters in her course (that is, those who
entered the Sisterhood at the same time as she did) told
us that from this day on something special shone forth

from Sister Claudia, as though she shared a personal secret with the Lord Jesus. She herself once said that at that time the Lord led her into a new sphere. From then on, she came to sense something of Jesus' grief, of His suffering because of sin. And it was really true. When Sister Claudia only heard or discovered that she or another Sister had grieved Jesus through their sin, she wept bitterly. I can still see her sitting in my room. There had been disappointment and distress caused by some of the Sisters. As we talked together about it, her answer came in sobs: "What have we done to Jesus!" In this particular case she was not involved, but because she was one with her Sisters, she felt just as guilty. In her love for Jesus she could not bear Him to be grieved through our sin.

At the beginning, she had been one of the "last" in our Sisterhood, for she was not sensitive to sin in her life and therefore lukewarm in her discipleship. But now she had become one of the "first". It was her faith in the power of the blood of Jesus which had brought about such a change. But would she really grow and become steadfast along this way? Would she really learn how to overcome her weaknesses and sins? After all, by nature she was impulsive and high-spirited, and at the same time she was touchy and easily discouraged. Her sin and weak nature literally became her gain, because she did not resign herself to her sins and weaknesses.

One day she wrote: "Now I have learned this. I won't just look at my sin, seeing what I am like and my great weakness. Even though a burning pain fills my heart because I have failed and grieved others, I will look beyond my sin, unto Jesus. Is He only supposed to help the strong? No. He helps the weak. Jesus, You say, 'Those who are well have no need of a physician, but those who are sick.'

12

I thank You from the bottom of my heart, for I come to You sick in spirit and soul, my Saviour, my Redeemer, my dearest Lamb of God."

That was the secret of her victory, of her transformation. Her sins drove her into the arms of Jesus. Her sins made her claim the blood of Jesus that cleanses us from all our sins and releases us from our bondages.

So it was that she truly fought a battle of faith, in all constancy—and she held out until the chains were broken. At first she didn't sense anything of this transformation. We could hardly see it either. But then it became evident that such a battle of faith, calling upon the blood of Jesus and in the commitment to humble oneself ever anew, is not in vain. Fuelled by her repentance, the flame of love in her heart became brighter and brighter. This made her strong—strong in love, strong to sacrifice and suffer. And she, who previously had always sought to avoid her cross, was now so captivated by Jesus' suffering that her own suffering became insignificant in comparison. She, who had once been weak and inconsistent, often taken up with human interests and desires, could now be happy when things were hard and bitter for her although previously these things would have depressed her.

In 1969 she was transferred to Rome, to one of our foreign branches. The parting from the Mother House and her beloved land of Canaan almost broke her heart. Later she said. "That was the hardest day of my life." She dearly loved Canaan, the Mothers and the Sisters. Shortly afterwards we promised she could come back to the Mother House for a special festival. She just lived for the day when she could return. But then it wasn't possible after all. It was hard for us to tell her this as we thought it would make her very sad. With anxious hearts we opened her letter of reply.

13

But then we read, "I am experiencing literally that Jesus makes bitter things sweet and changes the sorrow of being far away from the Mother House into peace and joy." And indeed she was very happy and comforted during this great disappointment, as the other Sister in the branch told us later. Although she was a "home-sick child", she was able to overcome her homesickness in Rome more and more until she could write in her diary, "My home is where You have placed me. I will find joy there, because it pleases You. O my Lord Jesus, I want to walk Your way alone; I want to follow you out of love . . . Prepare me for suffering . . ."

As we read her letter from Rome we were deeply moved. What releasing power lies in the blood of Jesus—when we believe in it! We were overwhelmed to see how love for Jesus has the power to change everything and make the bitter sweet.

Everything had indeed changed in Sister Claudia's life through faith in the power of the blood of Jesus and in His complete redemption. And it was this faith which brought her such a great love for Jesus. Through this love, shame was transformed into bliss. In the middle of the traffic turmoil in Rome, she once had to stand on a street corner waiting to cross the street. A car stopped next to her; a young man leaned out and looked contemptuously at the cross on her dress. Filled with hatred, he spat in her face. She wrote to us, "Great joy filled my heart, that I could suffer a bit of disgrace for my disgrace-laden Lord. Normally, it would have disgusted me, but He made the bitter sweet." That was the secret of her life: "Jesus makes bitter things sweet. This is my secret happiness."

But because this was her life, this secret became more and more manifest when "bitter things" struck her. So

Sister Claudia could even rejoice when she one day found herself standing between bare walls in their small flat in Rome. What had happened? Suddenly almost all the furniture our Sisters had borrowed was taken away from them. They hadn't had the faintest idea that this would happen. How were they to live in the almost empty apartment? They had no money to buy furniture. But the bitter had become sweet for Sister Claudia. Someone else might have resented this and been very troubled, but she cheerfully exclaimed, "Now we are true Franciscans!" and began to sing our Sister of Mary song:

How blessed, how blessed, they who are poor shall be!

It made her so happy: "We can be poor and go the way of our Lord Jesus." As a true child she trusted: "The Father will take care of us!" At the Mother House she had experienced how furniture was delivered unexpectedly and so the empty rooms could be filled. The same happened in Rome. Our Sisters' flat was soon refurnished.

By nature Sister Claudia was weak, yet when it came to troubles, she proved that instead of being overwhelmed by them she could overcome them triumphantly. This transformation is beyond human explanation, but the secret is revealed in Sister Claudia's diary. She wrote, "Because You, Lord Jesus, have cleansed me from so many sins through Your holy blood, my heart is overwhelmed with gratitude. That in turn makes me capable of everything."

The forgiveness of Jesus enabled her to commit herself to suffering out of love for Him, and later to fulfil this commitment. She really lived out the dedication that she wrote in her diary: "Yes, in blind obedience I want to prove my love for You. I want to live to do Your will. I want to renounce everything that binds me to this world. I renounce my drive to work for work's sake. I renounce my desire for recognition among the Sisters. I renounce my lukewarmness and indifference to the commandments and the Rule of the Sisterhood. I renounce the smallest thought which leads me to criticize the Word of God. I renounce the old nature in me that does not want to fight, believe, suffer, love, obey and serve humbly. I confess now before the visible and invisible world: there is no one in heaven or on earth who is greater, dearer or more desirable to me than God the Father; than Jesus the Son, our Saviour, Redeemer, Bridegroom, Judge and King; than God the Holy Ghost, the fiery Flame of heaven, the Spirit of God . . . If only I have You, I will not seek anything else in heaven or on earth . . ." And through God's leadings this commitment was put to the test.

Glory Comes Out of Deep Suffering

It came quite unexpectedly. In spring, 1970, the Lord brought suffering and illness into Sister Claudia's life. In the prime of life, especially strong and healthy, she was suddenly afflicted with a fatal blood disease. Once physically strong, she was now weak and helpless. Once glowing with health, never having known physical sickness, her body was now racked with pain. But because she had never been ill, Sister Claudia did not take the first symptoms seriously. She couldn't imagine that her fatigue and pains had a more serious origin. She thought she simply needed to overcome them. In love for Jesus she continued to make strenuous speaking tours in Italy. In her heart there burned a fire: "Jesus must be glorified. Him will I serve!" She spent herself completely for the Lord's sake. Paying no attention to her suffering and her troubles, she daily made many secret sacrifices. She lived out the words of the hymn she had copied into her diary:

> Jesus, Your life was an offering.
> O Lord, let my life be one too,
> Living and dying that others
> Might see, in me only You!

Then came the day when Sister Claudia had to go to the hospital in Rome, and the results of the tests indicated a blood disease. But because the diagnosis was not clear, the doctors advised her to return to the Mother House as quickly as possible. Sister Claudia was so happy to be home again that her health seemed to improve slightly. Overflowing with spiritual life in her love for Jesus, she

17

was eager to share in all the concerns of our commission, and of her Sisters, and all that was happening on Canaan. The Sisters could scarcely believe that she was seriously ill. Joy and love shone forth from her.

But the pains became worse and worse. Difficult nights followed. And still, the love for Jesus proved its power. Quite alarmed by the seriousness of her sickness, I sat by her bedside. But it was not her pains and suffering that were the topic of conversation. She wept bitterly over something else: so many people throughout the world were falling away from Jesus. She had seen much of this backsliding in Italy as well. Yes, even those who had consecrated their whole life to the Lord Jesus had become unfaithful to Him.

Some days later the doctor referred her to a specialist for blood diseases in a hospital in a different city. After a few days, we received an alarming telephone call. There was no more help for Sister Claudia. Her days were numbered. Mother Martyria and I were to tell her that she had only a limited number of weeks or days to live. How would she react to this news? We shall never forget that visit to the hospital. Just before our arrival the doctor had given her a hint that her illness was incurable. In addition she had had many sleepless nights filled with pain. With anxious hearts we opened the door. Our Sister Claudia looked up at us radiantly with an enchanting smile that was not of this world.

We shall never forget that moment: it will always remain in our hearts. The heavenly world, her Lord Jesus, had come to greet her and had laid His radiance upon her. It had happened during her flight home from Rome. She had written in her diary: "The plane flew towards the sun. All at once it seemed to me as though the Lord Jesus was asking me, 'And if this illness should lead to death?' O,

Jesus, in this moment You have filled my heart with such infinite longing that I can scarcely restrain the surging joy, soon, soon, to see You! Soon, soon, to embrace You! Will this flight home be a flight into the arms of my Lord? Will it be the bridal flight for me?"

Sister Claudia could only react in this way, because for a long time now with her growing love for Jesus her yearning to be with Him in heaven had also grown. Six months before her death, while she still felt perfectly fit, she had written even at that early date, "Let my love for You burn so brightly that soon You can come to fetch me home."

To drink in His loveliness—this was her yearning. So she did not have to stop and think when we asked her which Bible verse we should write for the wall of her hospital room. "I shall be satisfied when I awake, with thy likeness" (Psalm 17:15 A.V.). That was her desire.

As we sat by her bedside during our first visit to the hospital, she asked us openly, "How much time do I have left? I am not ready to die yet!" And when I answered, "You still have much to suffer; He is preparing you," her request was, "I only want to go home to Jesus as a beautifully adorned bride. Please pray for this and let all my Sisters pray that I may be prepared."

In her diary she wrote something like this: "My Lord Jesus, release me completely from every bondage, even the very smallest one that I still have in body, soul or spirit to earthly things. I yield myself completely and unconditionally to all pain and suffering that will release me from all earthly ties and prepare me for Your throne. O Lord, I ask for nothing less than to be with You eternally, worshipping Your wounds as the marks of Your victory, that have brought me salvation. Lead me into suffering so that in this short time I may still bear fruit for You." And then she

19

listed all her prayer burdens for Jesus' commission and His kingdom. Now she practised what she had written down as her goal at the beginning of that year, 1970, without knowing what would await her in the coming months: "I do not account my life of any value nor as precious to myself, if only I may accomplish my course" (Acts 20:24).

In the face of death our innermost being is revealed. And in Sister Claudia it was revealed that Jesus lived in her. She had no ulterior motive of bringing glory to herself. She was concerned only about Jesus, that He should receive love and glory. She paid little heed to herself and her pain. Jesus and His suffering filled her heart. And the suffering of Jesus was the source of her strength: her own suffering paled in comparison.

This she experienced during her last days in the hospital. Her letter is a precious document for us: "Yesterday I had an especially bad day. When the pains began in the morning, I suddenly heard within me Jesus' lament that the angel choir sang in the Gethsemane Play,* 'My strength is broken'. At first I lamented to Jesus in these words about my suffering." Then, however, Sister Claudia heard the lament of Jesus louder and louder in her heart and all her own suffering faded away and she continued, "What grace it is to taste a little misery that I may come closer to Him." Then it seemed to her as though she was singing with the choir, as she had done in previous years, "Glory comes out of deep suffering!" This anthem seemed to swell up without end, and all sang this song to Jesus as a mighty host. Sister Claudia closed her letter by saying, "I was immeasurably happy."

That was not just an emotional experience. Her whole being testified to how Jesus had made her strong and happy

*One of our Passion Plays.

in the midst of pain and temptation, which she was not spared. This she had already testified to in her genuine love for all the Sisters and in her work for our commission.

The specialist who treated her was very moved by the way in which she bore this fatal disease. He had never met such a reaction in any other patient, above all from someone so young. In other cases when he had had to inform patients of such a diagnosis, he had usually experienced reactions of despair. But Sister Claudia had responded with quiet confidence. Overwhelmed, he declared, "People who have faith in Christ have a rock upon which they can stand." And when she suffered such excruciating pain in the following weeks, the specialist and nurses couldn't understand where she derived her strength from. Not only was she able to endure everything bravely, but she was in complete peace in the face of death. She was radiant with divine joy.

Love for Jesus made her strong so that she did not shrink from suffering. For out of this love she had only one longing, one prayer—to glorify Jesus in her pain in complete dedication to the suffering that He placed upon her, and that He would count her worthy to enter the fellowship of His sufferings. So she suffered—as she testified in her diary—day and night united with Him, her beloved Lord Jesus.

In her last difficult days of suffering she thought about all the people today who want to deaden every pain at once, and wrote: "But that is not the way for me. I want to suffer for You to the extent that You give me the strength. Yes, I have this burning desire to suffer for You, my dearest Lord Jesus!" The Lord took her at her word and the last days brought her excruciating pain. The awareness of the presence of Jesus left her. She had to walk through the dark valley of pain, of death. But Jesus sustained her and gave her the strength to bear her suffering to the point of death with the one prayer that she might glorify Jesus through it. And this was granted to her.

Sister Claudia had one last fervent earthly wish which she laid before the Father time and again. It was her wish to die in the Mother House. And this the Lord fulfilled. A few hours before her death—up till then the doctors would not allow her to be moved—she was brought home from the hospital to Canaan. In those last hours of her life she was able to see her Sisters once more. She lay upon her bed in dreadful pain and agony, but still with a triumphant joy, filled with supernatural radiance. This joy overflowed to all the other Sisters who gently passed through her room to see her for the last time. She greeted each one with a warm and loving glance. At this time it was wonderfully manifest what her life actually consisted of—love for Jesus, the great joy in Him, which is stronger than everything else. The Lord called her to her eternal home just a few hours later. It was the day after Pentecost, 1970.

Our Sister Claudia, whose name meant "weeping", had gone to her eternal home, the land of joyful bliss and laughter. But our hearts were filled with deep grief. Mother Martyria and I had lost a dearly loved daughter and the loss for her Sisters was just as great, especially for those who were most closely connected with her. Still it was our experience—at the funeral and in the evenings afterwards when we spoke together about her—that the deep joy was much greater than the grief. Wonder and amazement filled our hearts, and we praised the Lord for what He had accomplished in His child to His glory. We could almost see her above in heaven, adoring the Lamb of God, rejoicing with inexpressible gratitude. Now she was allowed to behold the One whom her soul loved.

Sister Claudia has been taken from us, and yet she continues to live among us and many others. The life of Jesus in her has not died, but it continues to live and has already blessed countless people who knew her or heard about her; for her life revealed what Jesus' blood can accomplish. Once weak, she had become strong. Once afraid of suffering, she then was willing to suffer. Once wavering and unsteady, she then was dedicated and faithful. Once more or less indifferent towards Jesus, she had received a burning love for Him. Once depressed, she had become happy and radiant. She would often sing the song, "Who makes us happy, Jesus, as You! . . ." That was really her song.

Sister Claudia brought this joy to countless people, as many letters after her death testify. "We remember Sister Claudia only as the Sister of joy!" Or, "She left a ray of light and joy behind her. Her radiance reminded me more of the blessed joy of eternal life than the toilsome earthly pilgrimage. What impressed me so much was her radiant being."

Yes, the radiance that shone forth from her was so great at the end of her life that one of our older Sisters who sat across from her at the table said later, "I could scarcely believe that the radiance on a person's face could be so tangible, almost material." This was truly the wondrous work of the blood of the Lamb!

Sister Claudia's Prayer*

My dear Lord Jesus,

I ask You, prepare me so that I may love You as You would have me love You, that I may not disappoint You in anything. May I fulfil Your highest wish and love You as You desire to be loved by me, without any compromises, by loving nothing besides You, by letting nothing be greater or more important to me than You. May You alone and Your suffering set my heart aflame and nothing else. Reveal to me the secret of Your suffering and Your agony on the cross. Let me suffer with You out of compassion and bring You comfort. May Your suffering so fill my heart that I find nothing too hard. May I count all things as loss in comparison to Your suffering and the calling to comfort You.

Help me to renounce sin one hundred per cent and not to give in to the smallest, not even to the first, sinful thought so that I do not grieve You.

Grant me repentance ever anew even for the smallest sin. Let me always be conscious of my sin so that I may respond to Your love as a repentant Mary Magdalene, pouring out my love upon You in gratitude.

May You be my All and I a mere nothing in Your eyes and in the sight of men, so that You might live in me completely and shine forth from me. This is my prayer. Amen.

*On August 2nd, 1968, Sister Claudia asked for a prayer that would help her to come to a pure love for Jesus.